Harpers Ferry

The Story of

JOHN BROWN'S RAID

BY TRACY BARRETT

Spotlight on American History
The Millbrook Press • Brookfield, Connecticut

For Laura Beth
and Patrick

Cover photo courtesy of The Granger Collection
Photos courtesy of: Schomburg Center for Research in Black
Culture, New York Public Library: pp. 8, 16 (right), 18, 20,
23, 43; The Bettmann Archive: pp. 10, 12–13, 24, 26, 29, 30,
34 (center), 48–49, 56; West Virginia State Archives: pp. 16
(left), 41; Harpers Ferry National Historic Park: pp. 34, 37;
Metropolitan Museum of Art: p. 53; Photo 1, Inc.: p. 54.

Library of Congress Cataloging-in-Publication Data
Barrett, Tracy, 1955–
Harpers Ferry : the story of John Brown's raid / by Tracy Barrett.
p. cm.—(Spotlight on American history)
Includes bibliographical references and index.
Summary: Examines the personal background of abolitionist John
Brown and the events surrounding the raid he led on the United
States arsenal at Harpers Ferry, West Virginia, in 1859.
ISBN 1-56294-380-4 (lib. bdg.)
1. Harpers Ferry (W. Va.)—History—John Brown's Raid, 1859–
Juvenile literature. 2. Brown, John, 1800–1859—Juvenile
literature. [1. Harpers Ferry (W. Va.)—History—John Brown's
Raid, 1859. 2. Brown, John, 1800–1859. 3. Abolitionists.]
I. Title. II. Series.
E451.B27 1993
973.7′116—dc20   92-39810 CIP   AC

Published by The Millbrook Press
2 Old New Milford Road, Brookfield, Connecticut 06804

Contents

Harpers Ferry

1

DEATH AT HARPERS FERRY

John Brown watched helplessly as his youngest son, hit by a bullet, lay dying before his eyes. The young man begged his father to kill him, to put him out of his misery. His father finally said to him, "If you must die, die like a man." Oliver Brown tried to raise himself up, failed, and said, "It is all over with me." A few minutes later his father called his name and received no answer. "I guess he is dead," said Brown. When the fighting ended, according to an eyewitness, John Brown "walked to his son's body, straightened out his limbs, . . . [and] said, 'This is the third son I have lost in this cause.' "

John Brown, two of his sons, and other men had come to Harpers Ferry, Virginia, to try to end slavery in the United States by seizing the federal armory and using it as their base of operations to liberate the slaves of the area. They hoped that news of their "raid," as they called it, would spread quickly among the slaves in the South and inspire them to join their cause. But from the start, things had gone badly for the raiders.

Watson Brown, one of John Brown's older sons, had been shot earlier that same day, October 17, 1859, when his father had sent

In the midst of the battle at Harpers Ferry, John Brown feels the pulse of his son Oliver. Another son, Watson, lies dead at his feet.

him and another man out under a white flag of truce to negotiate a surrender. Instead of allowing the men to pass safely, riflemen sprayed them with bullets, wounding them both fatally.

Both sides were caught up in the intensity of the battle, and horrors were perpetrated on the combatants. Dangerfield Newby, the first of John Brown's men to be killed, was a former slave who had been trying desperately to earn enough money to buy his wife and six children out of slavery. When he heard that John Brown was going to attack slavery itself, he eagerly joined in the fight, only to be killed early on Monday morning. Spectators watched as his ears were cut off his corpse.

Finally, a troop of eighty marines stormed the building in which Brown and the surviving members of his party had barricaded themselves. At a signal by J.E.B. Stuart, later an important general in the Confederate Army, the marines broke down the door. Lieutenant Green was among the first to enter the building. He thrust his sword with all his strength in John Brown's side. Observers, seeing only the hilt and half the blade outside Brown's body, assumed that the rest of the sword had penetrated. The sword had really bent in two on Brown's belt, causing him pain and injury, but not killing him. Frustrated and enraged, Green grabbed his sword by its blade and beat Brown over the head with the hilt, again and again, until blood poured down the old man's face.

The raid was over. Seventeen people lay dead, including ten of Brown's followers, the mayor of the town, two slaves, and several townspeople.

What had inflamed the passions of these men so much that they were willing to sacrifice their lives and their families? What caused men to fight so viciously, killing truce-bearers and mutilating corpses? The answer lies in the passionate anti-slavery convictions of the raid's leader. He was variously known as Shubel Morgan, John Smith, and Osawatomie Brown, but history remembers him as he introduced himself to J.E.B. Stuart: "Old John Brown."

"VICTIM OF A TYRANT'S LASH"

*S*lavery existed in the Americas long before the first Africans were brought to these shores in chains. When the Spanish explorer Hernando Cortés traveled through Mexico in the early sixteenth century, he saw Indian slaves for sale in the marketplaces. Since the dawn of history, in fact, people have enslaved each other, often subjecting enemies captured in war or members of another ethnic group to this fate. The peoples of Africa were long victimized in this way, from ancient times all the way through the mid-nineteenth century. It is estimated that in the two hundred years between 1650 and 1850, more than twelve million Africans were taken from their homes and sold as property to slaveholders in Europe, the Americas, and other parts of Africa. Eventually, more slave labor was used in the southern United States than anywhere else in the world. After being kidnapped by slave traders or sold to the traders by other Africans, Africans were taken to America by ship on a journey of such hardship that about one out of five of them died. The survivors were sold to the highest bidder to work for no pay for the rest of their lives.

An American slave market.

For many centuries slavery was accepted as a normal condition; American slaveholders even found passages in the Bible to justify the system of slavery and the way they treated their slaves. But by the seventeenth century, people were beginning to question whether the practice was moral, and all over Europe, country by country began to outlaw the holding of slaves.

A slave shack in the South.

In the southern United States, however, the slavery system was deeply entrenched. And the condition of slaves there was grim indeed. In one small step toward the abolition, or ending, of slavery, in 1808 the United States government banned the importation of slaves from Africa, thus limiting the slave population to the people who had been born in bondage and their offspring. Southerners objected to this law since, as the Yazoo, Mississippi, *Democrat* put it, "the only practical means of perpetuating our present system of labor is by importing Africans." The domestic slave trade continued to thrive. In the early 1830s, field laborers sold for about six hundred dollars, with house slaves or skilled artisans selling for as much as one thousand dollars, and once in a while for even twice that amount. Since there were not enough slaves to go around, there were rumors that free blacks and sometimes poor whites were occasionally kidnapped and sold as slaves.

Children of a free father, either black or white, and a slave mother were considered slaves. The New York *Tribune* in 1858 reported one alleged case in which a father, an unnamed senator from Missouri, was aware that his nine-year-old daughter by a slave mother had been taken from her and sold to Mississippi; he even traveled on the same boat as his child. The *Tribune* reporter noted the hypocrisy of his position, saying, "Here was a child of tender age, torn from her mother, and doomed to a Mississippi plantation, while her father, in the august Senate of the United States, declaims of liberty. He stands coolly by, while his own child . . . is taken forcibly from her mother and driven off with a gang of Slaves to a distant land, among strangers, never again to know a mother's love or caress, but to be thenceforth the victim of a tyrant's lash, or lust."

In the face of such horrors as these, the abolitionist movement grew stronger, with many prominent people, both black and white, calling for the end of slavery. Some slave owners left wills freeing their slaves at their deaths, and others freed them in their lifetimes. The more farsighted of these took steps to educate and train their slaves before or after freeing them, knowing that liberty without the ability to earn a living was a further cruelty.

THE MAKING OF AN ABOLITIONIST

John Brown was born in Torrington, Connecticut, in 1800. When he was five years old, his family moved to what was then the wilderness of Ohio. John was enthralled by the Indians living nearby. He was afraid of them until he got his first lesson in the equality of the races from his father, who treated them as fellow human beings.

His mother died when John was a child. His father soon remarried, to a good, kind woman, but John never accepted her and mourned his mother's death for years. John's father, Owen Brown, was a stern, pious man, whose belief in the religious doctrine of Calvinism dominated his every waking moment. In Owen Brown's interpretation of the Bible, slavery was an abomination and a sin against God. In a letter written late in his life, Owen boldly declared, "I am an Abolitionist." He taught his children to be kind to black people, as they were their equals. He said that others treated them as inferior beings only because of their country's unjust laws and white people's prejudice. He was active in the Underground Railroad, a system of safe houses that offered protection to slaves along their escape routes from bondage.

John's father and mother.

John Brown never completely believed in his father's religion, saying he was only "to some extent a convert to Christianity." Although he did not belong for any length of time to a particular religion, he agonized later in his life over the lack of faith of several of his children. And the great abolitionist Frederick Douglass said of Brown, "Certainly I never felt myself in the presence of a stronger religious influence than while in this man's house."

Owen Brown was in the cattle business, and as a boy John had to herd cattle hundreds of miles from home to market. When he was thirteen, he drove a large herd to the house of a man who allowed him to stay with him a few days before returning home. There an incident greatly impressed John, accustomed as he was to his father's views on the equality of the races. He later told this story, in which he refers to himself in the third person.

During the war [of 1812], a circumstance occurred that in the end made him [John Brown] a most *determined Abolitionist:* & led him to declare, *or Swear, Eternal war* with *Slavery.* He was staying for a short time with a very gentlemanly landlord once a United States Marshal who held a slave boy near his own age very active, intelligent and good feeling: & to whom John was under considerable obligation for numerous little acts of kindness. *The master* made a great pet of John: brought him to table with his first company, & friends; called their attention to every little smart thing he *said or did;* & to the fact of his being more than a hundred miles from home with a company of cattle alone; while the *negro boy* (who was fully if not more than his equal) was badly clothed, poorly fed; & *lodged in cold weather;* & beaten before his eyes with Iron Shovels or any other thing that came first to hand. This brought John to reflect on the wretched; hopeless condition, of *Fatherless* & *Motherless* slave *children:* for such children have neither Fathers nor Mothers to protect, & provide for them. He would sometimes raise the question *is God their Father?*

From a young age, John Brown was deeply upset by the ill-treatment of slave children.

It would seem that the loss of his own mother led him to sympathize with a child his own age who had neither mother nor father to protect him.

At the age of nineteen, Brown briefly studied for the ministry, but an inflammation of the eyes prevented him from completing his studies, and he gladly went back home, where he soon married. His first wife was named Dianthe Lusk. She bore him seven children in the space of eleven years, although she was not in good health. Brown called her "remarkably plain" but a good, pious woman. She suffered from deep emotional problems, and when she died giving birth to their last child in 1832, she was said to be insane.

John Brown needed help raising his many children, and barely a year after Dianthe died, he married seventeen-year-old Mary Ann Day, with whom he had thirteen children, seven of whom died young. In all, seven sons and four daughters lived to maturity. While the loss of nine of his children was painful to the family, in the early nineteenth century and especially in the sparsely settled regions of the country, many children died before their fifth birthdays. Still, John Brown was unusually devoted to his children, and when he buried one ten-month-old baby girl, whom he himself had nursed through her final illness and who was extremely attached to him, he broke down and wept. Once in the space of a few days, he lost four children to dysentery and was quite ill himself. He often took care of his sick children himself, staying up many nights in a row to nurse them.

He was an unusually stern father, but he tried to be fair, too. When his children were older, he wrote to his wife, "If the large boys do wrong, call them alone into your room and expostulate [reason] with them kindly, and see if you cannot reach them by a

Family Record.

DEATHS.

Owen Brown (Father of John Brown) died May 8th 1856 Aged 85 Years

Frederick Brown died 31st March 1831 Aged 4 Years

Dianthe Brown died 10th Aug. 1832 (Infant Son buried with her) Aged 31 Years n t died Aug 7th 1832

Charles Brown died 11th Sept 1843 Aged 5 Years

Austin Brown died 21th Sept 1843 Aged 1 Year

Peter Brown died 22d Sept 1843 aged 2 Years

Sarah Brown died 23d Sept 1843 aged 9 Years

Amelia Brown died 30th Oct 1846 Aged 16 Months

Ellen Brown died 30th April 1849 Aged 11 Months

Infant Son died 17th May 1852 Aged 21 days

Frederick Brown 2d was Murdered at Osawatomie in Kansas Aug 30th 1856 Aged 26 years

In a span of twenty-five years, Brown lost his first wife and their infant son, eight young children, a twenty-one-year-old son, and his father.

kind but powerful appeal to their honor." In his day, when physical punishment of children was the rule, John Brown's thoughtful words were revolutionary. His children, although afraid of his severity when they were young, remained devoted to him throughout their lives.

Meanwhile, Brown's anti-slavery feelings were growing. During his lifetime there were many attempted slave uprisings, some of them successful. The island republic of Haiti was established in 1804 after an extremely bloody slave revolt toppled the white rulers. In this way, the first country governed by blacks in the Western Hemisphere was born. Brown was a great admirer of the revolution's leader, Toussaint L'Ouverture. Nat Turner's Virginia slave revolt of 1831, while bloody and short-lived, inspired many people who thought that the only way to rid the United States of slavery was through armed warfare. Other people, including Denmark Vesey, plotted armed insurrection, only to be discovered before they could carry it out.

John Brown at first tried peaceful ways to oppose slavery. He wanted to educate slaves and former slaves, for he knew that freedom without means for support would scarcely be an improvement over bondage. He and his friends wanted to raise money to buy slaves, educate them, and free them, but he soon realized that at current prices (six hundred dollars and up per slave) they could not make a dent in the slave population. He tried to change his neighbors' attitudes. At one point he brought blacks into his church to sit at his family pew, but this only led to his expulsion from the church. He also wished to improve on the Underground Railroad and make it more efficient, but since its very nature depended on secrecy, it was difficult to get its "conductors," as people involved in it were called, to work together. Then in 1839, John Brown swore "active war on slavery."

Brown knew that he could not free the slaves of America by himself. He needed a trained group of followers. In his quest for supporters, he made a strong impression on many of the people who met him. The author of *Two Years Before the Mast*, Richard Henry Dana, Jr., was on a walking tour in 1849 when he stumbled on the cabin where Brown then lived in upstate New York. Brown invited Dana and his companion, who were unaware of their host's identity, to stay for a meal. In his journal, Dana describes "that plain, bare farm, amid the blackened stumps, the attempts at scientific agriculture under such disadvantages, the simple dwelling, the surveyor's tools, the setting of the little scene among grand, awful mountain ranges, the negro colony and inmates, the family bred to duty and principle, and held to them by a power [John Brown] recognized as being from above." He also noticed with amazement that not only did two "negroes" join them at the table, but Brown addressed them as "Mr." and "Mrs.," a courtesy not customarily extended to blacks at that time.

Two years earlier, in 1847, Frederick Douglass, who was a dedicated pacifist, came close to changing his peaceful views after meeting Brown. "From this night spent with John Brown," he later said, "while I continued to write and speak against slavery, I became all the same less hopeful of its peaceful abolition." It was at this meeting that Brown told Douglass about his secret plan to end slavery: He and a group of followers would raid the fields of the South, liberating slaves as they went.

Brown did not forget the need for slaves to take an active part in their own liberation. In 1847 or 1848 he wrote a pamphlet called "Sambos Mistakes," in which he took the voice of a slave who regretted his lack of education and knowledge of slave revolts. He urged slaves to stop "licking the spittle [spit] of a Southerner," to rise up against their oppressors, the people who ruled over them.

FREDERICK DOUGLASS

By the time John Brown met him in 1848, Frederick Douglass was a well-known abolitionist speaker. He had been born a slave around 1817 on the Eastern Shore of Maryland, an area known, like Harpers Ferry, for its "humane" treatment of slaves. But the experiences he relates in his autobiographies (the best known is *Narrative of the Life of Frederick Douglass*) are filled with the horrors he wit-

nessed as a child and young man. He had the luck to be sent to Baltimore as a child. Although it was illegal for slaves to learn how to read and write, this did not stop the determined and intelligent Douglass from teaching himself. He managed to escape from servitude to freedom in the North in 1838.

Frederick Douglass's rare powers as a speaker were discovered at an abolitionist meeting three years later, and he quickly became a spokesperson for the anti-slavery movement, touring the northern United States and Britain to speak against slavery.

Douglass's involvement in equal rights for blacks did not end with the start of the Civil War. Too old to fight himself, he was an influential recruiter for the Union cause, and after the war he worked closely with the government to establish equal rights for all citizens. He died in 1895.

Toussaint L'Ouverture,
the leader of the successful
Haitian slave revolt, was
an inspiration to Brown.

He also began to study tactics of revolution. While on a business trip to Europe in 1851, he took the time to inspect battlefields and fortresses. He began to read a lot, studying those times in history when oppressed peoples made war on their oppressors. He was especially interested in ancient Rome and its slave population, and he also learned about the Jews' rebellions against their Egyptian masters in Biblical times.

THE SHEDDING OF BLOOD

The people of the United States could not agree whether slavery should be allowed to continue in their country. Many people, mostly in Northern cities where slave labor was not important to the economy, argued that the system was cruel and that the government should outlaw slavery. Others, mostly in the rural South, which depended on slaves to work the plantations, said that individual states should be allowed to decide for themselves whether or not to allow slavery. In an effort to please both sides, the federal government, when declaring Kansas and Nebraska territories in 1854, said that the people who lived there would be able to decide for themselves if this large area would be free or slave. Instantly, people on both sides of the issue flooded the region in order to vote either for or against slavery. Five of John Brown's sons went to Kansas; two of them merely wanted to settle in the newly formed territory, but three saw it as a chance to fight slavery. In 1855, John Brown entered the territory, and within a week he and his sons went to guard voters on election day against threats by pro-slave advocates—that is, those who supported the system.

FREE STATE CONVENTION!

All persons who are favorable to a union of effort, and a permanent organization of all the Free State elements of Kansas Territory, and who wish to secure upon the broadest platform the co-operation of all who agree upon this point, are requested to meet at their several places of holding elections, in their respective districts on the 25th of August, instant, at one o'clock, P M., and appoint five delegates to each representative to which they were entitled in the Legislative Assembly who shall meet in general Convention at

Big Springs, Wednesday, Sept. 5th '55,

at 10 o'clock A M., for the purpose of adopting a Platform upon which all may act harmoniously who prefer Freedom to Slavery. The nomination of a Delegate to Congress, will also come up before the General Convention. Union and harmony are absolutely necessary to success. Let no sectional or party issues distract or prevent the perfect co-operation of Free State men. And to contend against them successfully, we also must be united— pro-slavery party are fully and effectually organized. No jars nor minor issues divide them. Let every man then do his duty and we are certain of victory. Without prudence and harmony of action we are certain to fail. Let immediate and effective steps to insure a full and correct representation for every District in the Territory.

All Free State men, without distinction, are earnestly requested to this immediate and effective steps, as per resolution of the Mass Convention in session at Lawrence, since in the Territory.—Unless we stand, divided we fail.

C. ROBINSON, Chairman.

By order of the Executive Committee of the Free State Party of the Territory of Kansas.
Herald of Freedom, Print.
Aug 1st and 16th, 1855.
J K GOODIN, Sec'y

Brown and his sons were among the people who answered the call to fight for Kansas to become a free state.

He then went back home and traveled around making speeches about the abolitionist cause. At one meeting, he told his listeners that "without the shedding of blood there is no remission of [release from] sins." He returned to Kansas in 1856 to join in the increasing conflict between pro-slave and anti-slave factions.

Both sides harassed each other in an attempt to scare off voters. Thousands of men from the slave state of Missouri poured over the border into Kansas to influence the vote. One group of pro-slavers was particularly troublesome, terrorizing local settlers, setting fires, and threatening anti-slave advocates. On May 24, 1856, at Pottawatomie Creek, Kansas, Brown and four of his sons, his son-in-law, and two other men, rounded up five men whom they saw as the worst offenders and killed them. People later claimed that not only were these men innocent, but some of them were actually against slavery. Brown maintained to his dying day that he did not actually kill anyone at Pottawatomie, but there is no doubt that he gave the orders that led to their deaths.

From the time of these violent events, which became known as Bleeding Kansas, Brown was a hunted outlaw, and he would remain so to the end of his days. With a band of men, he kept up his anti-slavery work in Kansas, using tactics of secrecy and surprise. A few months after the Pottawatomie massacre, a messenger told him that the town of Osawatomie was under attack by Missourians and that his son Frederick had been killed defending the town. Brown led his troops into battle. They were greatly outnumbered, though, and were forced to retreat and watch helplessly as Osawatomie burned to the ground. It was here that he acquired the well-known nicknames Captain Brown and Osawatomie Brown.

Years after these events, his half-brother Jeremiah R. Brown wrote, "Previous to this he had devoted himself entirely to business, but since the Kansas troubles he has abandoned all business and become wholly absorbed in the subject of slavery."

Although Brown had apparently given up all hope of abolishing slavery by peaceful means, he still wished to ground his rebellion in the law. Since he was an outlaw in the United States, he chose Chatham, Canada, as the place to read to a select group of forty-five black and white abolitionists his "Declaration of liberty by the Representatives of the Slave Population of the United States of America." He quoted heavily from the American Declaration of Independence, saying his aim was to "secure equal rights, privileges, & Justice to all; Irrespective of Sex; or Nation." This forty-eight-article declaration called for the abolition of slavery, good treatment of prisoners, immediate founding of schools and churches, and other social reforms. His views on the equality of blacks and whites were radical, and so was his insistence that men and women be treated equally. The Emancipation Proclamation freeing the slaves was signed in 1863, but women—white and black—were not given the vote in the United States until 1920.

THE BEECHER FAMILY

The Beecher family, eleven children headed by the remarkable Reverend Lyman Beecher, was deeply involved in the abolitionist cause. The most famous member of the family was Harriet, who wrote the novel *Uncle Tom's Cabin* (published in 1852). Although it has been criticized in this century for its depiction of slaves as childlike and innocent, this book did much to inflame the anti-slavery feelings of Northerners and Southerners alike. When Abraham Lincoln met Harriet Beecher Stowe in 1862, he remarked, "So this is the little lady who made this big war." In Europe at the time of the Harpers Ferry raid, she wrote that the harsh measures meted out by the slaveholders in the wake of the raid would not "subdue the tremor caused by [Brown's] great quiet spirit."

Her brother Henry Ward Beecher was known as an inspiring preacher, and when he turned his considerable talents to the abolitionist cause, his eloquence won many converts. His Plymouth Church in Brooklyn was the most famous in America, regularly attracting more than the three thousand people it could hold. His writings attacking slavery were as rousing as his sister's. In spite of his abolitionist sympathies, Beecher did not support John Brown's raid at Harpers Ferry. He called Brown "a crazed old man." But he did make a dramatic statement about Brown's execution, when he brought into Plymouth Church the chains that had bound Brown on his way to the gallows. As his anti-slave congregation shouted their rage at slavery, he trampled on the chains, all the while calling for the end of slavery.

The Beecher brothers and sisters were united in their hatred of the unequal treatment of human beings in their day.

Henry Ward Beecher and Harriet Beecher Stowe

JOHN BROWN

Although other people would later criticize this document as being contradictory in some places and unclear in others, to his abolitionist followers, whom he called delegates, this was unimportant. As one recent writer has put it, "Their trust was not in Brown's paperwork, it was in the man. They saw in him a firebrand, 'the man to do the deed if it must be done,' as he was characterized by the schoolmaster-philosopher Bronson Alcott." The black delegates also apparently did not object to the fact that all the executive positions in Brown's new "government" were filled by whites.

John Brown planned to make the goals of this declaration come true by striking a blow at slavery. In order to start the process of freeing the slaves, he would seize the arsenal (where weapons were stored) at Harpers Ferry. When news of the raid spread, he expected, according to Richard Realf, who was present at the meeting, "that all the free negroes in the Northern States would immediately flock to his standard [banner]. He expected that all the slaves in the Southern States would do the same. He believed, too, that as many of the free negroes in Canada as could accompany him, would do so."

Once he had a large army of black and white followers behind him, Brown planned to place squads in the hills surrounding Harpers Ferry. Brown and his men would hide from the authorities, and occasionally he would send his most persuasive followers down to the outlying plantations to encourage the slaves there to join him. For this reason, the logical time for the raid to take place would be in the spring, when the loss of even a small part of the working slave population would be devastating to the farmers.

After his trip to Canada, Brown returned to Kansas with a small band of recruits, where he waited for money and more supporters to reach him. Hiding his true identity under the alias of Shubel

Morgan, he stayed there six months. During this time a black man named Jim Daniels asked Brown to rescue him, his family, and a friend from slavery in Missouri. Brown and his followers crossed over the border and took eleven slaves at gunpoint from two different houses, killing a slave owner in the process. They then took horses, oxen, food, and bedding. John Brown said that this was not theft; to his mind these goods were owed to the slaves, since they had worked all their lives without pay. The slaves hid in a farmhouse for a month, waiting for the search to die down, and then they left for Ontario, Canada. They were forced to travel very slowly, since it was bitterly cold, and a baby named John Brown Daniels had been born during the month of concealment. It took them eighty-two days to cover about one thousand miles. They finally reached their destination in March 1859.

THE RAIDERS

Brown's plan was a daring and dangerous one, and although he had many admirers, he found it difficult to convince them to join him. Many people who hated slavery as passionately as he did were still not convinced that the only way to end it was through violence. Others disapproved of his plan; they thought it was bound to fail. He did, however, manage to persuade twenty-one men to enlist.

Three of them were his sons. Oliver, his youngest boy, was a tall, strong twenty-year-old who had just been married. Watson, twenty-five, was also tall and strong, whereas Owen, thirty-five, had been a sickly child. He was described as "partially crippled, good-tempered and cynical."

John Brown's right-hand man was twenty-four-year old John Henry Kagi, a white man who had been one of his early recruits. Kagi was handsome and well educated, and had long been an active abolitionist.

John Brown's first black recruit was Shields Green, whose nickname was Emperor because of his aristocratic bearing and because of a rumor that he was the descendant of an African prince.

Oliver Brown

John Brown

Watson Brown

HARPERS FERRY RAIDERS

Shields Green

John Henry Kagi

Dangerfield Newby

John Brown

John A. Copeland

[34]

He became a runaway slave when his wife died, and he joined Brown's group soon afterward.

Dangerfield Newby had been a slave but was freed. His wife and six children, however, were left in bondage. He was trying to earn enough money to buy their freedom. His young wife, who missed him terribly, wrote him long letters begging him to return. Possibly the realization that he would never be able to earn enough money to free his family made him decide to take the desperate step of joining in Brown's raid.

Lewis Sheridan Leary, a freeman, was a well-educated man who belonged to a debating society. He was the uncle of the fifth of Brown's black recruits, John A. Copeland, who stood firm in his resolution to fight for the end of slavery. Shortly before he was executed, Copeland would say: "I am not terrified by the gallows, which I see staring me in the face, and upon which I am soon to stand and suffer death for doing what George Washington was made a hero for doing."

John Brown was by this time fifty-nine years old. He had grown a long, white beard to help disguise him—he was, after all, still a fugitive from the law. He was five feet nine inches tall, with black hair and striking steel-gray eyes. People who knew him said he was humorless and austere. An acquaintance described him as follows: "I looked up and met the full, strong gaze of a pair of luminous [glowing], questioning eyes. . . . It was a long, rugged-featured face I saw. A tall, sinewy figure, too. . . . The impression left . . . was that of reserve, endurance, and quiet strength. . . . The mouth . . . looked like that of a man who was swift to act." When he walked, "Every one gave way; a crowd parted like the waters when a strongly-driven boat presses through."

These were the men who came to Harpers Ferry, Virginia, in 1859.

SETTING THE STAGE

Virginia would be on the Confederate side during the Civil War, but in 1862 its anti-slave citizens would secede, or withdraw, from Virginia to form the free state of West Virginia. Harpers Ferry is located on what is now the eastern tip of West Virginia, at the lowest altitude of that mountainous state. It sits on a point of land formed by the joining of the Potomac and Shenandoah rivers. Different Native American tribes occupied the area off and on before the arrival of white people. The first documented white settlers arrived in 1733, although there are some stories of whites in the area before. In 1734, Robert Harper arrived and established a ferry across the Potomac River. From then on it was known as Harper's, or Harpers, Ferry.

On a tour of Virginia, Thomas Jefferson explored this region and said that the sight of the mountains rising out of the rushing water was "one of the most stupendous scenes in nature" and that it was "worth a trip across the Atlantic."

River trade helped the town grow, although it expanded slowly until 1796 when a federal armory was established there. In 1819, Halls' Rifle Works was set up on an island in the Shenandoah. Hall

"View of Harpers Ferry, Virginia (from the Potomac side),"
by Currier & Ives.

had invented the breech-loading flintlock rifle, an important development in firearms, but his factory, slow to adopt modern machinery, failed to keep pace with its Northern competitors. Still, the armory and the rifle-works increased the town's importance, and in 1836, after the railroad had arrived, a striking Y-shaped bridge was built over the Shenandoah. This aided the river trade, and the small town grew and prospered. By the mid-nineteenth century, Harpers Ferry counted between 2,500 and 3,000 inhabitants, including 1,252 free blacks and 88 slaves. Many of the white people were Northerners who had come south to work at the rifle factory. The city had become an important link in trade and transportation between the eastern and western United States.

Most of the buildings in Harpers Ferry were made of rough local stone or brick. They were crowded along the two main streets and included an impressive Roman Catholic Church in the Gothic style that had been built in 1830. Much of the town would be destroyed by both Union and Confederate troops, which occupied the town at various times during the Civil War. Afterward, Harpers Ferry would be chosen (in part, no doubt, because of its historic significance) for the site of Storer College, whose aim would be to educate the recently freed black population.

The area around the town is still ruggedly beautiful, and it is easy to see why Brown chose it for his raid. The many caves in the hills offered excellent hiding places both for runaway slaves and for the guerrilla bands that Brown intended to command. There were also many streams and ponds so that people in hiding would have plenty of water. In addition, Harpers Ferry lay very close to the Mason-Dixon line, which would make it relatively easy for slaves to cross over to the North. The presence of the arsenal was probably the final reason that Brown chose Harpers Ferry for his raid.

[38]

It was guarded by civilians, not soldiers, and would thus be easy to capture. He hoped that the weaponry stored there would soon be at his disposal.

On the other hand, the slaves in Harpers Ferry had had plenty of chances to escape in the past, and they had rarely done so. Writing after the raid, an abolitionist Methodist minister who lived in the area said that the slaves "were generally well-cared for and contented. Being close to the free soil of Pennsylvania they could have gotten there in a night had they wished to escape bondage, and then they could have easily reached Canada by the Northern Aid, called the 'Underground Railroad.' " As to Brown's idea that the slaves would come flocking to the arsenal, he said, "A more idiotic and senseless theory never entered an American mind." Whatever the reason, the slaves did not join the rebellion. This would prove disastrous for the raid.

Brown was aware of the risks of his plan but insisted that even if the raid failed, news of it would inspire others to join the anti-slavery movement. His sons tried to dissuade him but to no avail. Finally Oliver said, "We must not let our father die alone," and he convinced Watson and Owen to join him.

7

TO THE ARSENAL

John Brown planned to attack Harpers Ferry immediately after the Chatham Convention, but lack of money and the loss of his British drillmaster Hugh Forbes (who quit after several months with no pay) forced him to postpone his raid. He tried to recruit other well-known abolitionists to join, but he met with some resistance. After a meeting with Frederick Douglass in August 1859, Douglass wrote in his journal, "Brown for Harpers Ferry and I against it—he for striking a blow that should instantly arouse the country, and I for the policy of gradually and unaccountably drawing off the slaves to the mountains, as at first suggested and proposed by him." While people in contact with Douglass after the raid said that he supported it, Douglass himself always denied this, saying that he had advised Brown not to attempt violence.

Harriet Tubman, the famous conductor on the Underground Railroad, had met Brown in 1858. Although she had at first said she would join the fight, in fact, she did not. She told Brown that she was ill and so unable to attend. Historians have since wondered if she had actually decided that the raid was not consistent with her non-violent method of hastening the end of slavery and used her well-known poor health as an excuse.

Other people had concerns about Brown and his ideals as well. Two Quaker brothers were in support of Brown and abolition yet were worried that Brown would not survive the raid. One of them wrote an anonymous letter to Secretary of War John B. Floyd, to "protect Brown from the consequences of his own rashness." He told Floyd that John Brown was planning a raid at a federal arsenal, but mistakenly said that the arsenal was located in Maryland. For some reason, Floyd failed to recognize that John Brown was Osawatomie Brown, the man still wanted by the law for his part in the Kansas troubles. Since there was no arsenal in the state of Maryland, he decided the letter was a hoax and failed to act on it.

An artist who met John Brown in August 1859
drew this sketch of the two of them together.

Meanwhile, Brown had changed his original plan. Instead of holing up in the mountains, he and his thousands of expected followers would move southward, sending armed parties into the countryside to liberate more slaves. Those who wished to join in the fight would do so, while those who preferred to flee to Canada would be assisted in their flight. He would strike more arsenals, gathering weapons, until the upheaval he expected to follow would complete his work.

John Brown arrived in Harpers Ferry on July 3, 1859. Taking the name Isaac Smith, he said he was in the cattle business. He later rented a farm known as the Kennedy place and told people that he intended to start a mining operation. He even sent men out in the hills with picks and shovels, pretending to prospect. They made offers to buy some of the surrounding farms, further diverting suspicion from their plans as the excited landowners thought about possible profits rather than insurrections.

His recruits began trickling in. It was difficult to hide their traces in the house, so he called for his daughter-in-law Belle (Oliver's wife) and his youngest daughter, Annie, to come down from North Elba, New York, to keep house for them. The black raiders and most of their white counterparts had to spend much of their time concealed upstairs in the small farmhouse, being careful not to make any noise when neighbors came to call.

In an old log cabin, John Brown began amassing an impressive amount of firearms. According to Samuel Leech, the Methodist minister who lived in the area, at the time of the raid he had "200 Sharpes' rifles, 13,000 pistol caps, 40,000 percussion caps, 250 rounds of powder, 12 reams of cartridge paper and other warlike materials."

The Kennedy place, where Brown and his men hid out before the raid.

John Brown had already postponed his raid from springtime to fall. He intended to wait until the end of October for the actual attack. Reinforcements would arrive at that time, since Brown did not want to draw attention to his group by flooding the area with men until they were actually needed. Yet for some unknown reason, on Sunday, October 16, 1859, he called his men together and told them to ready themselves for the raid that night. He warned them solemnly, "Consider that the lives of others are as dear to them as yours are to you. Do not, therefore, take the life of anyone, if you can possibly avoid it; but if it is necessary to take life in order to save your own, then make sure work of it."

Why did he change his mind and attack before his much-needed men and supplies could arrive? There is no certain answer to this question. The fact that a slave in Harpers Ferry, despondent over the sale of his wife to a distant location, had hanged himself that week, may have convinced John Brown that local slaves would be angry enough to join him more readily than they might otherwise have been.

In any case, Brown and his followers left the Kennedy farm around midnight that Sunday. It was cold and overcast, with a light rain and no moon to light the way. The little band of sixteen whites and five blacks moved as quietly as they could down the dirt road, armed with pikes, sledgehammers, and crowbars. As they went they cut the telegraph wires linking the area to Washington and Baltimore.

Brown, confident that local slaves were eager to join him, took hostages along the way to the arsenal, intending to exchange them later for black men willing to fight. Among the first hostages taken was George Washington's great-grandnephew, Colonel Lewis W. Washington. According to Osborne Anderson, the slaves they met along the way were overjoyed at the news of the insurrection and blessed them for leading it. None, however, joined them as they continued on their way.

The group forced its way into the armory, capturing the guard. They armed the bewildered slaves that they found there. Then they settled in to wait, with the sixty hostages they had seized, for the arms that they had stockpiled on the farm.

"WAR IN THE STREETS"

All this time, the group had worked in near silence, taking hostages by surprise and confining them so as not to let word of the raid spread. But one of the hostages, a guard named Patrick Higgins, knocked down his captor, Oliver Brown, and ran away. One of the raiders fired a shot at him, but it just grazed him, and he continued his escape, alerting the townspeople. The first fatality, ironically, was a free black man. He was Heyward Shepherd, a railroad employee. Unaware of what was transpiring at the arsenal, he wandered into the area. When he realized that there was trouble, he turned to flee and spread the alarm, but one of Brown's men shot and killed him as he ran.

The townspeople were becoming aware that violence had erupted in the area. A local marine paymaster, John E. P. Daingerfield, was awakened by one of his servants, who told him that there was "war in the streets." When he went out, he found that the streets were empty. Exploring further, he stumbled on the raiders, who seized him as a hostage and kept him for the duration of the raid. He later recalled, "During the day and night I talked much with John Brown, and found him as brave as a man could be, and sensible upon all subjects, except slavery. Upon that question he was a religious fanatic, and believed it was his duty to free the slaves, even if in doing so he lost his own life." Daingerfield said that throughout that night and the next day, he often saw Brown stop his followers from shooting at unarmed men.

Since the telegraph wires had been cut, no one outside the area was as yet aware of what was happening. A freight train pulled into the train yard and was instantly fired upon by the raiders. It stayed waiting in the yard, unable to move forward or back, until Brown gave the order to allow it to move on. The engineer did so with all possible speed, and at every stop spread the news. People began pouring in from all over the area, and the militias of Maryland and Virginia were alerted.

All this time, Brown was anxiously awaiting the men and weapons that he had left at the farm. They were delayed in coming, and as the townspeople became aware of the raid, his situation grew more and more dangerous. Brown's men urged him to flee, but as he looked out the window anxiously, he refused, saying that now that they were there, they had to see it through. When the hostage Daingerfield told Brown he was committing treason by his actions, two of the raiders turned to him in surprise. They asked Brown if this was true, saying that they had no intention of fighting against their country. He insisted it wasn't, but they were not satisfied, and would probably have deserted if they hadn't been afraid for their lives.

As people flooded the town on Monday, October 17, the situation deteriorated. Men broke into saloons, according to Higgins (who had escaped safely), then armed themselves and "kept shouting, shooting at random, and howling." The mayor of the town, who had always supported blacks in Harpers Ferry, went unarmed into the open area near the arsenal, only to be shot and killed by one of Brown's men. When his will came to be read after peace had been restored, it was found that he had ordered his five slaves liberated after his death—the only slaves freed by the action at Harpers Ferry.

More intense fighting broke out as the militias of Maryland and Virginia arrived. John Henry Kagi, who was holding the rifle works along with John Copeland, was killed, and Copeland was captured. The youngest raider, twenty-two-year-old William Leeman, leaped out a window and tried to run away, only to be gunned down as he reached the Potomac River.

Before noon, eighty marines led by Robert E. Lee attacked the arsenal as Brown and his followers retreated to the engine house, a small brick building on the arsenal grounds. They barred themselves in and drilled small holes through the bricks for windows.

On the morning of Tuesday, October 18, seeing that Brown's situation was hopeless, Lee sent his emissary J.E.B. Stuart to the arsenal to ask for his surrender. Brown refused, unless he and his men would be given safe passage out of the area. Stuart said this was impossible and then suddenly leaped back from the open door and waved his hat as a signal to his troops. A group of marines leaped at the door, which was instantly slammed shut and barred. The marines picked up a ladder and, using it as a battering ram, pounded the door over and over until it burst open. Lieutenant Green leaped at Brown, stabbed him, and hit him over the head. The surviving raiders, some of them seriously wounded, were captured. By noon on Tuesday, October 18, John Brown's raid at Harpers Ferry was over. Seventeen men lost their lives. Five raiders escaped, including Owen Brown, who had been stationed outside the arsenal and fled when hearing of the raid's failure.

*Marines led by
Robert E. Lee
stormed the arsenal.*

*A day and a half after
the fighting had begun, all
but five of the raiders were
either killed or captured.*

Brown lay on the floor. Alexander R. Boteler, who had seen the fight, went in to talk to him. Boteler later said, "On entering the room where John Brown was I found him alone, lying on the floor on his left side, and with his back turned toward me. The right side of his face was smeared with blood from the sword-cut on his head. . . . . I . . . asked the question: 'Captain, what brought you here?'

" 'To free your slaves,' was the reply.

" 'How did you expect to accomplish it, with the small force you brought with you?'

" 'I expected help.'

" 'Did you expect to get assistance from whites as well as from the blacks?'

" 'I did,' he replied.

" 'Then,' said I, 'you have been disappointed in not getting it . . . ?'

" 'Yes,' he muttered, 'I have—been—disappointed.' "

"JOHN BROWN'S BODY"

John Brown's trial was speedy. He was captured on Tuesday and his trial was on the following Friday. His lawyers initially pled insanity in an attempt to keep him from the gallows, but he indignantly refuted them and said that he was as sane as they were. The court agreed with him, and on the next Monday, after the jury had deliberated for less than an hour, he was found "Guilty of treason, and conspiring and advising with slaves and others to rebel, and murder in the first degree." Each of these crimes carried the death penalty.

At his arrest, he was asked if he had anything to say. Unprepared to speak at this time, he nonetheless made an eloquent statement of his position, saying in part, "Two of my sons were killed here today, and I'm dying too. I came here to liberate slaves, and was to receive no reward. I have acted from a sense of duty, and am content to await my fate; but I think the crowd have treated me badly. I am an old man. Yesterday I could have killed when I chose; but I had no desire to kill any person, and would not have killed a man had they not tried to kill me and my men. . . . If I had succeeded in running off slaves this time, I could have raised twenty times as many men as I have now, for a similar expedition. But I have failed."

While in prison, Brown received many visitors, including Virginia's Governor Wise, who said, "He is a bundle of the best nerves I ever saw. . . . He is a man of clear head, of courage, fortitude, and simple ingenuousness. He is cool, collected, indomitable, and . . . he was humane to his prisoners, . . . and he inspired me with great trust in his integrity, as a man of truth. He is fanatic, vain, and garrulous, but firm and truthful, and intelligent."

In his last letter to his children, Brown begged them to "abhor, with undying hatred . . . , that sum of all villanies, slavery." On the day of his death, Brown wrote, "I John Brown am now quite *certain* that the crimes of this *guilty land: will* never be purged *away;* but with Blood. I had *as I now think: vainly* flattered myself that without *very much* bloodshed, it might be done."

On his way to the scaffold, Brown said to the jailer accompanying him, "This is a beautiful country. I never noticed it before." Among the witnesses to his execution was a young soldier in the Virginia militia named John Wilkes Booth. He was to become the assassin of Abraham Lincoln.

As soon as he was dead, legends began to spring up concerning Brown. A New York *Tribune* reporter wrote that as Brown was leaving the jail to be executed, "a black woman, with her little child in her arms, stood near his way. He stopped, for a moment, in his course, stooped over, and, with the tenderness of one whose love is as broad as the brotherhood of man, kissed it affectionately." Witnesses to the execution denied that this incident ever took place, but it instantly captured the public's imagination.

Thomas Hovenden's "The Last Moments of John Brown"
portrays Brown as a kindly, tragic figure.

*John Brown, who towers over clashing Union and Confederate
troops, helped to ignite the flames of Civil War.*

The town of Harpers Ferry was in shock. The slave owners clamped down on their slaves, forbidding them to meet with each other. Despite this new harshness, the slaves held secret meetings, and reports of arson against white property began to filter in, along with news of the mysterious deaths of livestock that had previously seemed healthy. The white people thought, probably correctly, that their slaves and the free blacks of the region were causing this damage. The rest of the country was in an uproar, with most of the newspapers in both the North and the South condemning the raid. In the South, people suspected of being abolitionists were tarred and feathered, whipped, and even lynched. Some abolitionists who had previously been pacifists now encouraged others to take a more active part in the destruction of slavery. The prominent newspaper publisher William Lloyd Garrison had been strongly opposed to any sort of violence until the raid, but then he said, "as a peace man—I am prepared to say: 'Success to every slave insurrection at the South, and in every slave county.' . . . Rather than see men wearing their chains in a cowardly and servile spirit, I would as an advocate of peace, much rather see them breaking the head of the tyrant with their chains."

The reaction abroad was mostly in favor of the raid. The French author Victor Hugo wrote an editorial saying, "In killing Brown, they have committed a crime which will take its place among the calamities of history. The rupture of the Union will fatally follow the assassination of Brown. As to John Brown, he was an apostle and a hero. The gibbet [gallows] has only increased his glory, and made him a martyr."

The other captured raiders were eventually executed, although with less haste than their leader. While they received less attention than John Brown, they also had the sympathy of much of

[55]

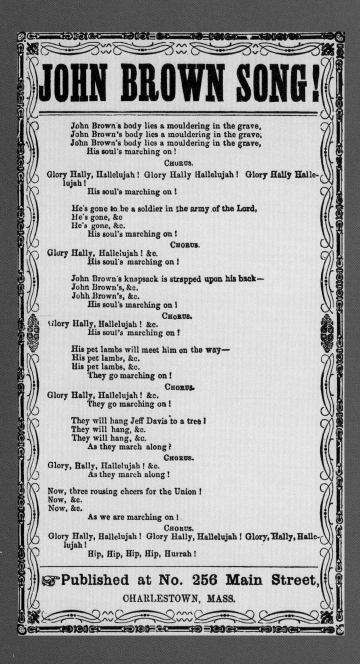

JOHN BROWN SONG!

John Brown's body lies a mouldering in the grave,
John Brown's body lies a mouldering in the grave,
John Brown's body lies a mouldering in the grave,
His soul's marching on!

CHORUS.

Glory Hally, Hallelujah! Glory Hally Hallelujah! Glory Hally Hallelujah!
His soul's marching on!

He's gone to be a soldier in the army of the Lord,
He's gone, &c
He's gone, &c.
His soul's marching on!

CHORUS.

Glory Hally, Hallelujah! &c.
His soul's marching on!

John Brown's knapsack is strapped upon his back—
John Brown's, &c.
Johh Brown's, &c.
His soul's marching on!

CHORUS.

Glory Hally, Hallelujah! &c.
His soul's marching on!

His pet lambs will meet him on the way—
His pet lambs, &c.
His pet lambs, &c.
They go marching on!

CHORUS.

Glory Hally, Hallelujah! &c.
They go marching on!

They will hang Jeff Davis to a tree!
They will hang, &c.
They will hang, &c.
As they march along?

CHORUS.

Glory, Hally, Hallelujah! &c.
As they march along!

Now, three rousing cheers for the Union!
Now, &c.
Now, &c.
As we are marching on!

CHORUS.

Glory Hally, Hallelujah! Glory Hally, Hallelujah! Glory, Hally, Hallelujah!
Hip, Hip, Hip, Hip, Hurrah!

☞**Published at No. 256 Main Street,**
CHARLESTOWN, MASS.

[56]

the public. Admirers, both black and white, raised money for the support of their families, and a large sum of money came in from Haiti.

In a speech given at the foundation of Storer College, established after the Civil War at the site of the raid, Frederick Douglass said, "If John Brown did not end the war that ended slavery, he did, at least, begin the war that ended slavery." Others have argued that he was a madman, a bloodthirsty killer who seized upon the issue of slavery as an excuse to commit wholesale slaughter. In either case, he did at least achieve his goal of capturing people's imagination and inspiring them to join in his crusade. Union soldiers marched into battle to the tune of "John Brown's Body," and his death was used as an example of the evils of a slaveholding society.

Brown was buried near a huge boulder on his family farm in North Elba, New York. He is still admired by many believers in equal rights, and his home and the town of Harpers Ferry are visited by many wishing to pay their respects to the man that they believe struck the first real blow in the fight against slavery in the United States.

These are the original words of "John Brown's Body," sung by Union soldiers during the Civil War.

Chronology

1800	May 9	John Brown is born in Torrington, Connecticut.
1821	June 21	Marries Dianthe Lusk.
1832	August 10	Dianthe Lusk dies.
1847		Visited by Frederick Douglass.
1855		Goes to Kansas.
1856	May 23–26	Pottawatomie murders.
1858	May 19	Chatham Convention.
	December	Rescues slaves from Missouri.
1859	July 3	Arrives at Harpers Ferry.
	October 17–18	The raid.
	December 2	John Brown is executed.

Further Reading

Bains, Rae. *Harriet Tubman: The Road to Freedom*. Mahwah, N.J.: Troll Associates, 1982.

Marsh, Carole. *Out of the Mouths of Slaves*. Decatur, Ga.: Gallopade Publishing Group, 1989.

McKissack, Patricia, and Fredrick McKissack. *Frederick Douglass: The Black Lion*. Chicago: Childrens Press, 1987.

Meltzer, Milton. *All Times, All Peoples: A World History of Slavery*. New York: HarperCollins Books, 1980.

Scott, John A., and Robert A. Scott. *John Brown of Harper's Ferry*. New York: Facts on File, 1988.

Sterne, Emma G. *The Slave Ship*. New York: Scholastic, 1988.

Bibliography

The quotations that appear in this book are drawn from among these sources.

Anderson, Osborne P. *A Voice from Harper's Ferry*, in *The Black Heritage Library Collection*. Freeport, N.Y.: Books for Libraries Press, 1972.

Anti-Slavery Society. *The Anti-Slavery History of the John-Brown Year; Being the Twenty-Seventh Annual Report of the American Anti-Slavery Society*. New York: Anti-Slavery Society, 1861.

Daingerfield, John E. P. "John Brown at Harper's Ferry: The Fight at the Engine-House, as Seen By One of His Prisoners," in *Century Illustrated Monthly*, June 1885, pp. 265–267.

DuBois, W. E. Burghardt. *John Brown*. Philadelphia: George W. Jacobs & Co., 1909.

Hinton, Richard J. *John Brown and his Men, with Some Account of the Roads They Traveled to Reach Harpers Ferry*. New York and London: Funk & Wagnalls, 1894.

Leech, Rev. Samuel Vanderlip. *The Raid of John Brown at Harpers Ferry as I Saw It*. Washington, D.C.: The De Soto, 1909.

Oates, Stephen B. *To Purge This Land With Blood: A Biography of John Brown.* Amherst: University of Massachusetts Press, 1984.

Quarles, Benjamin. *Allies for Freedom: Blacks and John Brown.* New York: Oxford University Press, 1974.

Sanborn, F. B., ed. *The Life and Letters of John Brown, Liberator of Kansas, and Martyr of Virginia.* 1885.

Williams, John Alexander. *West Virginia: A Bicentennial History.* New York: W. W. Norton and Co., 1976.

Wilson, Hill Peebles. *John Brown, Soldier of Fortune: A Critique.* Lawrence, Kans.: Hill P. Wilson, 1913.

Index